BALLET OF THE
ELEPHANTS

★

BY LEDA SCHUBERT

ILLUSTRATED BY ROBERT ANDREW PARKER

A DEBORAH BRODIE BOOK
ROARING BROOK PRESS
NEW MILFORD, CONNECTICUT

To everyone at the Vermont College MFA in Writing for Children, who gave me courage;
to my writing group, who heard it first; to Lauren Wohl, Robert Andrew Parker, Deborah Brodie,
and Steven Chudney, who made it happen; and most of all, to my husband, Bob.

And in memory of my parents, who first took me to the ballet and the circus.
—L. S.

For Judy.
—R. A. P.

Art note: The art for this book was prepared in watercolor and ink on various papers.

Text copyright © 2006 by Leda Schubert   Illustrations copyright © 2006 by Robert Andrew Parker   A Deborah Brodie Book
Published by Roaring Brook Press   Roaring Brook Press is a division of Holtzbrinck Publishing Holdings Limited Partnership   143 West Street, New Milford, Connecticut 06776
All rights reserved   Distributed in Canada by H. B. Fenn and Company, Ltd.
Library of Congress Cataloging-in-Publication Data   Schubert, Leda.   Ballet of the elephants / Leda Schubert ; illustrated by Robert Andrew Parker.— 1st ed.
p. cm.   "A Deborah Brodie Book."   ISBN-13: 978-1-59643-075-4   ISBN-10: 1-59643-075-3   1. Circus polka (Choreographic work : Balanchine) I. Parker, Robert Andrew, ill.
II. Title.   GV1790.C57S34 2006   796.8'42—dc22   2005002670
Roaring Brook Press books are available for special promotions and premiums. For details, contact: Director of Special Markets, Holtzbrinck Publishers.
Book design by Jennifer Browne   Printed in China   First edition May 2006
10 9 8 7 6 5 4 3 2 1

In April 1942,
for two days and two nights,
a special train, fifty-five cars long,
traveled from Florida,
the winter home of the circus,
to New York.
From dawn until noon,
circus cars rolled from the railroad yards
to Madison Square Garden.

Lions roared
and monkeys argued.
Trapeze artists,
daredevils,
acrobats,

and one hundred clowns
paraded through the streets.
So did camels, llamas, zebras,
burros, hundreds of horses,

and fifty elephants. Fifty!
Children stayed home from school to watch.

The enormous elephants,
taught by Walter McClain,
the most talented trainer of his time,
were cared for by the circus bull men.

The elephants would perform in a ballet
dreamed up by John Ringling North,
owner of The Greatest Show on Earth;
arranged by the greatest choreographer
of the twentieth century,
George Balanchine;

with music by
the most famous
composer,
Igor Stravinsky.

This is how it happened.

John Ringling North
grew up in Wisconsin,
with five wild uncles
who owned a circus.
Johnny had wild ideas, too.

Once, he even brought a pony
up to the attic of an uncle's house.

In the summers, he rode
in his uncle's fancy private railroad car,
and he sold popcorn in the stands.
Before long, he was running the circus.
He was a showman with a vision
for a new kind of circus.
It would be spectacular.
One plan involved George Balanchine.

George Balanchine
was born five months
after John Ringling North,
in St. Petersburg, Russia,
a city of palaces,
a city that is famous for its white nights,
in June, when the sky is never dark.
A city as magical
as the circus itself.

When Balanchine was only nine,
he was sent away
to the Imperial Ballet School.
He learned to leap and turn,
and studied the piano.
He missed his family
and hardly ate at all.
Once he ran away.
But when he danced
in *The Sleeping Beauty*,
he fell in love with ballet.
At only nineteen,
he became ballet master
of the Mikhailovsky Opera Theater.
Like John Ringling North,
he had big ideas.

So did Igor Stravinsky, who loved to write music.
He, too, grew up in St. Petersburg,
delighting in its sounds:

droshkies rolling down the streets,
bells ringing from cathedrals,
women singing on their way
home from work.
His father sang opera.

The music Stravinsky wrote
had jarring rhythms and clashing sounds.
It shocked audiences.
It didn't sound like anything they knew.
At the world premiere of
The Rite of Spring,
his music for a ballet,
people hissed after the first chord.
Fistfights broke out in the audience.

Stravinsky said his music
was best understood by
children and animals.

Balanchine and Stravinsky
never met in St. Petersburg,
but when they settled in America,
they became friends.
They spoke to each other in Russian.

They created dances
that let the audience
see the music and hear the dance.
They loved Broadway theater
and Hollywood movies.

At a Broadway show,
Balanchine met Vera Zorina,
born in Germany,
who first danced on stage
as a butterfly
when she was six.
Balanchine fell in love,
and created dances
just for her.

One was a water ballet for a movie.
Zorina emerged from a pool
filled with white lilies
and appeared to dance on water,
Then she perched
on a giant statue
of a white horse.
Soon she would be perched
on a much larger animal.

John Ringling North
was dazzling audiences
with dreamlike images,
high-wire acts, and pageants,
but he had an idea.
He wanted to present
a ballet for elephants.
He called Balanchine.

Balanchine called Stravinsky.
"What kind of music?" asked
Stravinsky.
"A polka," Balanchine said.
"For whom?"
"For some elephants."
"How old?"
"Very young."
"All right," said Stravinsky.
"If they are very young, I'll do it."

Balanchine and Zorina
went to Florida
to study how
elephants moved.
Rehearsals began.
The elephants responded
to taps, voices, movement,
and food.
They worked for weeks.
Stravinsky sent the music.
It sounded like elephants:
sometimes heavy and slow,
with drums and trumpeting;
sometimes bright,
with piccolos and cymbals.
It ended with a march.

On opening night,
blue and red sawdust
covered the three rings.
Modoc, the largest Indian elephant
in America,
danced alone
lifting one foot and then another,
turning and turning.

Zorina joined her in a waltz.
At the end, they bowed
and touched foreheads
in the blue sawdust.

Then Modoc lifted Zorina
and carried her backstage,
curled in her trunk.
Zorina stroked Modoc's eyelid
and scratched the sole of her foot,
to thank her for the thrill.

The ballet followed.
Fifty elephants from the *corps de ballet*,
with Modoc as prima ballerina,
held each other by the tail,
dancing in an endless chain
through the three circus rings.
They raised enormous legs
to rest on each other's backs,
and trumpeted to Stravinsky's
odd harmonies.

They wore fluffy pink tutus
and jeweled headbands.
Their crowns glittered
as they moved their gigantic feet
and swayed their long trunks
in time to the music.
The ground shook.
Fifty ballerinas, young,
also in pink tutus,
but with only two feet,
danced with the elephants.

For a few minutes,
big dreams came true.
For the dazzled crowds,
Circus Polka was unforgettable.
The ballet had 425 performances.

Later, it was staged with people
instead of elephants.
But how could it have been as grand?

ABOUT THIS BOOK

Although I was dragged kicking and screaming into the wonderful world of tooth flossing, this book is the happy result. During my daily two minutes of flossing, I turn on the TV. One of the (only) four stations we receive is PBS, which one night rebroadcast a documentary about Balanchine originally produced in 1984. I saw elephants and I heard the words "choreographed a ballet." I threw down my floss (still haven't found it) and became obsessed.

I love elephants—their mystery, magnificence, and intelligence. I love ballet—I danced as the Sugar Plum Fairy in first grade. Little did I know what else I would come to love during my research, all as magical as elephants: St. Petersburg with its white nights and palaces, Stravinsky's music, Balanchine's history, and the strange story of John Ringling North. I lost myself in research, but it was many, many drafts before I found a way to tell the story and link the disparate pieces.

I am a librarian and I majored in history many years ago, so doing the research was exciting, even though I never left Vermont. I read biographies and autobiographies, as well as critical works about Stravinsky, Balanchine, North, and circuses. I used online resources to locate reviews of the circus as it happened from *The New York Times*. I used Web sites to investigate everything from photographs of St. Petersburg to the 7,000 yards of cloth used to make tutus for the elephants. I bought old copies of *Life* magazine on eBay.

Zorina in Modoc's trunk on opening night.
Herbert Gehr / Getty Images

After I had finished the manuscript and it was accepted for publication, I learned of another resource: the Popular Balanchine project, directed by Claude Conyers, currently located at the New York Public Library for the Performing Arts in New York City. <http://www.nypl.org> A dossier compiled by Sally Banes in April 2002 (amended December 2003), includes a full report on the ballet and several interviews that confirmed information I had found. Included was the 1942 circus route book, which reported that

- ★ the circus toured 104 cities;
- ★ it required 15 acres for the tents and circus yards;
- ★ during the entire tour, the elephants drank 534,000 gallons of water;
- ★ 4,120,000 people attended all 425 performances.

Balanchine rehearsing with Modoc.
Bettman / Corbis

An interview with Jerul Dean (aka Mary Lee) also mentioned that the elephants, even when they retired, so loved the ballet and were so well trained that they performed it all by themselves, without music.

Everything in this story is true (to the best of my knowledge). What's not in the story is that circus animals were sometimes mistreated. Any abuse of elephants breaks my heart, but many zoos and circuses now treat their elephants extremely well.

Finally, while several sources suggest that for Balanchine and Stravinsky the ballet was farcical, I am sure that was not true for the millions of children and adults who were fortunate enough to see it. After all, Balanchine himself said he was "an entertainer, a circus man" (Charles M. Joseph, *Stravinsky and Balanchine*, page 169).

The ballet of the elephants

Circus World Museum, Baraboo, Wisconsin

FURTHER INFORMATION ON CIRCUSES

The Ringling Brothers Circus Web site discusses both circuses and animal welfare at <www.ringling.com>. Specific information on the treatment of elephants can be found at:
<http://www.ringling.com/animals/elephant/perform.aspx>.

Scigliano, Eric. *Love, War, and Circuses: The Age-Old Relationship Between Elephants and Humans.* Boston: Houghton Mifflin Company, 2002.

Also visit: <https://www.circusworldmuseum.com>.

FURTHER INFORMATION ON JOHN RINGLING NORTH (1903–1985) AND CIRCUS HISTORY

Culhane, John. *The American Circus: An Illustrated History.* New York: Henry Holt and Company, 1990. (The conversation between Stravinsky and Balanchine is on page 243 and is also reported in several other sources.)

Hammarstrom, David Lewis. *Big Top Boss: John Ringling North and the Circus.* Urbana: University of Illinois Press, 1992.

Life magazine, April 20, 1942.

The New York Times: April 4, 5, 10, and 19, 1942. ProQuest Historical Newspapers.

FURTHER INFORMATION ON GEORGE BALANCHINE (1904–1983) AND IGOR STRAVINSKY (1882–1971)

George Balanchine choreographed more than four hundred ballets and was universally acknowledged as the foremost choreographer of his time. Many of his ballets have become classics, including his choreography for *The Nutcracker.* Stravinsky wrote music for thirty-nine of Balanchine's ballets.

The premiere of Stravinsky's *Rite of Spring* is widely thought to be the birth of modernism. Though Stravinsky's works were frequently controversial during his lifetime, parts of *The Rite of Spring* are on the Voyager spacecraft, currently on its way out of our solar system. The Voyager "Golden Record" is intended to portray the diversity of life on Earth.
<http://voyager.jpl.nasa.gov/spacecraft/music.html>.

"Stravinsky said his music was best understood by children and animals" is widely quoted, but may have originated in *Observer*, October 8, 1961.

Buckle, Richard, and John Taras. *George Balanchine: Ballet Master.* New York: Random House, 1988.

Joseph, Charles M. *Stravinsky and Balanchine: A Journey of Invention.* New Haven: Yale University Press, 2002.

Mason, Francis. *I Remember Balanchine.* New York: Doubleday, 1991.

PBS DVD: *American Masters: George Balanchine.* Kultur: 2004.

Zorina, Vera. *Zorina.* New York: Farrar, Straus and Giroux, 1986. (Zorina's reaction to riding Modoc is in this book.)

The George Balanchine Foundation <www.balanchine.org> is a particularly helpful site for information on Balanchine.

For information on St. Petersburg (with photos of the white nights):
<http://www.saint-petersburg.com/history/index.asp>.